Illustrations by Quan Mapps

ISBN: 979-8-9894468-0-3

Visit our website: www.sugarquartzspa.com

THIS NOTEBOOK BELONGS TO:

———————————❤———————————

Look at you...
Making it happen!
No need to overthink it.
You were born with everything
you already need.
You can't control everything.
So just let it come.
Let it go. Then let it flow.

CREATED BY: JASMINE MAPPS
ILLUSTRATED BY: QUAN MAPPS

NOTE TO SELF

Today is a good
day to reset.

TAKE
THAT
BREAK

MY NOTES

MY NOTES

MY NOTES

MY NOTES

DO SOMETHING
TODAY THAT YOUR
FUTURE SELF WILL
THANK YOU FOR.

Made in the USA
Columbia, SC
11 February 2024

744f8590-b17b-4459-983c-a20a9db2a8f2R02